Maria Tallchief

Terry Barber

FIRST NATIONS SERIES

Maria Tallchief is published by
Grass Roots Press, a division of Literacy Services of Canada Ltd.

www.grassrootsbooks.net

ACKNOWLEDGEMENTS

We acknowledge the financial support of the Government of Canada through the Canada Book Fund (CBF) for our publishing activities.

Produced with the assistance of
the Government of Alberta, Alberta
Multimedia Development Fund.

Alberta
Government

Editor: Dr. Pat Campbell
Image research: Dr. Pat Campbell
Book design: Lara Minja, Lime Design Inc.

Library and Archives Canada Cataloguing in Publication

Barber, Terry, date, author
        Maria Tallchief / Terry Barber.

(First Nations series)
ISBN 978–1–77153–045–3 (paperback)

        1. Tallchief, Maria. 2. Ballerinas—United States—Biography.
3. Indian ballerinas—United States—Biography. 4. Osage Indians—
United States—Biography. 5. Readers for new literates. I. Title.
II. Series: Barber, Terry, 1950– . First Nations.

PE1126.N43B36459 2015   428.6'2   C2015–904587–8

Printed in Canada.

Contents

Maria leaps across the stage.

A Star on Stage

Maria is out of breath. She takes in more air. Maria feels better. Maria sets her feet. She runs across the stage. Maria looks like she can fly. She leaps. Maria leaps into the arms of her partner. The crowd gasps.

People clap at a ballet.

A Star on Stage

Maria's dance partner holds her. Maria's head is close to the floor. The dance ends. The crowd loves Maria. They stomp their feet and clap. They yell: "Tallchief! Tallchief! Tallchief!" Maria never forgets how the people call her name.

Osage Chief White Eagle.
1934.

Early Years

Maria grows up in Oklahoma. She grows up on a **reservation**. The **Osage** have oil on their reservation. Some Osage are well off because of oil. Many Osage don't have to work because of oil. Maria's father is Osage.

Maria is born on January 24, 1925.

Maria's father.

Maria's mother.

Early Years

Maria loves her parents. Her father is a tall, good-looking man. Mostly, Maria feels safe with her father. Maria's mother is a tiny, pretty woman. Maria's mother wants the best for her family. She knows hard work makes life better.

Maria's mother's parents are Scottish and Irish.

Maria (left) dances with her sister, Marjorie.

Early Years

Maria's younger sister is named Marjorie. She and Maria are best friends. They dance together. Maria starts ballet lessons when she is three. Maria also plays the piano. Music and dance are part of her life.

Maria as a young ballerina.

A child swings from a tree.

Early Years

Maria loves to spend time outdoors. She loves to walk in her big yard. She loves to sit on the swing. Maria loves the garden. She loves to watch the horses. Maria loves to hunt for **arrowheads** in the grass.

Maria's ballet teacher is Madame Nijinska.

Maria's Teachers

Maria is 12 years old. Her family now lives in California. Maria has a new ballet teacher. Maria loves to dance. Maria decides to quit piano lessons. Maria wants to become a ballerina. Maria works hard.

Madame Nijinska helps a student.

Maria's Teachers

Maria's ballet teacher is strict. Elbows must bend a certain way. Fingers must point a certain way. Ballerinas must breathe a certain way. Ballerinas must sleep a certain way. Ballerinas stand tall no matter where they are. Ballet becomes Maria's life.

Maria trains with Madame Nijinska for five years.

A Ballet Russe poster for a French ballet.

Maria's Teachers

Maria moves to New York City. She is 17 years old. She works for a ballet company. For the first time, Maria is paid to dance. Maria has great talent. Maria also knows that hard work will make her the best. Maria works harder than ever.

The ballet company is called Ballet Russe.

George Balanchine watches Maria practise.

Maria's Teachers

In New York, Maria meets a new teacher. His name is George and he is one of the best. George helps Maria become stronger. Maria's body becomes stronger. Maria's mind becomes stronger. Like many dancers, Maria has great strength.

George talks to Maria.

Maria's Prince
of Dance

George starts a ballet company. He still teaches Maria. Maria is 20 years old. George is twice Maria's age. Each day, Maria learns more from him. Then things change. George falls in love with Maria. George asks Maria to marry him.

George's ballet company is called the Ballet Society.

George and Maria work together for years.

Maria's Prince of Dance

Maria cannot speak. George wants to marry her? Maria's parents think George is too old. George is twice divorced. Soon, Maria begins to see George as more than a teacher. She begins to see George as her "prince of dance."

George and Maria on their wedding day.

Maria's Prince of Dance

Maria and George marry in 1946. They sail to France. The French love ballet. Can an American Indian dance ballet? Yes, she can. The French love Maria's free and open style. Their eyes follow Maria's every move. Maria "dances like a flame."

Maria puts on her Osage headdress.

The Prima Ballerina

Maria is proud to be Osage. She is proud of her Native American blood. Maria says: "The American Indian wants to dance. They want to move." But Maria wants to be seen as a ballerina. She does not want to be called an American Indian ballerina.

Maria, the Prima Ballerina.

The Prima Ballerina

Maria joins George's ballet company in 1947. George sees in Maria her gift of dance. George creates ballets for Maria only. Maria finds the **roles** hard. George is patient. Maria never gives up. She learns the roles. Maria becomes a **prima ballerina.**

Maria takes a rest.

The Prima Ballerina

Hard work makes Maria a prima ballerina. Maria is often tired. Her muscles often hurt. Maria practises day after day. Often, she dances for crowds twice a day. Maria often works 14-hour days. Sometimes, Maria gets tired. But she never tires of dance.

Maria **poses** with her dance partner.

The Prima Ballerina

A prima ballerina is a star. She is the best ballerina in her ballet company. Maria gets the best roles. Maria gets to dance alone. Maria also dances with the best male dancers. Maria is one of the best ballerinas in the world.

Maria and Buzz on their wedding day.

Family and Fame

After five years together, Maria and George divorce. They remain friends. Maria keeps learning from George.

Maria falls in love with another man. His name is Buzz. They marry in 1956. Maria and Buzz have a baby girl.

Maria looks at her baby, Elise.

Maria is on the cover of Newsweek Magazine.

Family and Fame

Maria's fame grows. Her face is on the cover of magazines. She receives many awards. The Osage tribe names her Princess Wa-Xthe-Thonba. This means "Woman of Two Worlds." Maria enjoys the fame. She gets to meet many important people.

Maria works with a student.

Maria Passes the Torch

Maria starts to teach ballet. Maria is a tough teacher. She wants her students to do their best. Maria's best teachers made her work hard. Now, she wants her students to do the same. Maria passes on what she knows.

Maria retires from dancing when she is 40.

A young student gives Maria roses.

Maria Passes the Torch

Maria dies in 2013. She is 88 years old. When Maria dances, people love to watch. When Maria is asked to dance the impossible, she does. Maria's students learn to do the same. Maria's love of dance still **inspires** dancers today.

Glossary

arrowhead: the tip of an arrow.

inspire: to motivate.

Osage: a member of a North American Indian people.

pose: the way one stands or sits before someone takes their photo.

prima ballerina: the most important female dancer in a ballet company.

reservation: land set aside for North American Indian people.

role: part played by a person or thing in a particular situation.

Talking About the Book

What did you learn about Maria Tallchief?

What do you think Maria sacrificed to become
a prima ballerina?

What does "Wa-Xthe-Thonba" mean?
Why did the Osage give Maria this name?

The last chapter is called Maria Passes the Torch.
What do you think this means?

Picture Credits